SPIRIT *is* THICKER *than* BLOOD

A Memoir of Faith, Survival, and Redemption

— *by* —

Jamonica M. Gregory

This is a work of nonfiction. The events, experiences, and reflections shared in this book are based on the author's personal life. Certain names, details, or identifying characteristics may have been changed to protect the privacy of individuals.

All Scripture quotations, unless otherwise indicated, are taken from the Holy Bible.

The views and opinions expressed in this book are those of the author and do not necessarily reflect the official policy or position of any organization, employer, or institution.

TABLE OF CONTENTS

PREFACE & DEDICATION

This book is for the ones who have known pain intimately.

For those who were shaped by broken homes, strained relationships, and wounds that were never meant to be carried so young. For those who have wrestled with rejection, confusion, silence, and the quiet ache of not feeling fully seen or understood.

This is for every person who has faced life's challenges—especially the kind that come through family—and yet, by the grace of God, chose not to give up.

You may have been overlooked.

You may have been hurt.

You may have had to grow up faster than you should have.

But you are still here.

And that means something.

This story is a reminder that pain does not have the final word. That what tried to break you does not get to define you. That through faith in God, there is healing, there is restoration, and there is a path forward—even when it feels impossible.

If you have ever questioned your worth, your purpose, or whether your story could ever be redeemed, I pray this book meets you where you are and reminds you of this truth:

God sees you.

God knows you.

And God is not finished with you yet.

I also dedicate this book to the people God

has placed in my life as living proof of His love and faithfulness.

To my wonderful husband, A.C. Gregory—

Thank you for your patience, your covering, your strength, and your unwavering commitment to truth. Your love has been a reflection of God's grace in my life, and I am forever grateful for the way you lead, support, and stand beside me.

To my three beautiful daughters, Anna, Abigail, and Angel—

You are my miracles, my joy, and my daily reminder of God's goodness. Everything I am becoming, I pray will pour into you. May your lives be rooted in truth, covered in love, and guided by faith.

To my very special "sisters in love"—

Thank you for your support, your encouragement, and the bond we share. Your presence has been a gift, and I honor the love we walk in together.

And to my entire Spirit & Truth family—

Thank you for standing on the Word of God, for walking in truth, and for being a community built on love, accountability, and faith. You are more than a group—you are a family, and I am grateful to be part of what God is building through each of you.

This book is more than my story.

It is a testimony of what God can do with a life that has been broken, surrendered, and rebuilt in His hands.

And if He did it for me—

He can do it for you....

"For I am not ashamed of the gospel, because it is the power of God that brings salvation to everyone who believes.... "Romans 1:16 NIV

CHAPTER 1

LOST AND ALONE— "LEFT BY PEOPLE. HELD BY GOD."

When my father and my mother forsake me, then the Lord will take me up." Psalm 27:10

My story does not begin with me. It began with a little girl who's life was framed by loss.

My mother was only five years old when her world unraveled. She would remember that season in fragments: unfamiliar faces, hushed voices, the heaviness in the air when adults thought children could not feel what was happening around them. Lupus had taken her mother, and her father was already a mystery—a man whose absence had shaped her life before she was old enough to understand what fatherlessness meant.

She asked the question only a child could ask, simple and devastating.

"My mama's gone?"

"Yes," her older sister told her softly.

No one explained death in a way a five-year-old could hold. But my mother understood enough to know that the one person who should have been there to comfort her was the very one she had lost. She was too young to name grief, but not too young to feel abandoned by it.

After her mother died, she and her sisters were sent to live with an aunt. The house was full, but it was not tender. There was noise, responsibility, movement—but not the kind of love that makes a child feel safe. My mother learned early how to make herself small, how to stay out of the way, how to read the emotional weather in a room before speaking. Survival became her first language.

At night, she lay awake listening to the sounds of adults in other rooms, straining for some trace of comfort that never came. Sometimes she whispered into the darkness, as if heaven might lean down and answer her.

"Mama, where are you?"

But the room stayed quiet.

After a year, she and her sisters were moved again, this time to their grandmother's house. It was steadier there, less harsh, less uncertain. But even the most stable home cannot erase the ache of a child who has lost both mother and father in different ways. A grandmother's care could help her endure, but it could not replace what had been taken.

So my mother grew up with a wound at the center of her life—a wound made not only of grief, but of absence. She learned to keep going without the steady love every child deserves. She learned to function without belonging. She learned to live without being fully loved.

And in time, she became a mother herself.

A child who grows up without parents often enters adulthood carrying invisible fractures. Some people inherit land, stories, or wealth. My mother inherited survival. She pieced together motherhood from scraps—discipline she had seen, routines she had learned, instincts sharpened by hardship. She gave what she could, but what she had to give had been shaped by loss.

As her daughter, I often felt the sharp edges of that inheritance.

There were moments I longed for softness and did not find it. Moments when I wanted to be understood and wasn't. Moments when love felt present, but difficult to reach. As a child, I did not know how to separate my mother from the pain she carried. I only knew how it felt to stand on the receiving end of it.

But adulthood has a way of widening your vision.

Now when I look at my mother, I do not only see the woman who raised me. I also see the little girl she once was—the child who lost her mother before she knew how to spell her own name, the girl who moved from house to house searching for stability, the young woman who had to become strong long before she ever had the chance to feel safe.

And my heart softens.

That softening does not erase the pain. It does not rewrite difficult memories or pretend the wounds were not real. But it does give them context. It reminds me that my mother did not parent out of fullness; she parented out of survival. She gave what she knew. And much of what she knew had been forged in deprivation, not abundance.

So I choose forgiveness.

Not because nothing hurt, but because I finally understand that pain often travels through generations until someone names it, grieves it, and lays it down before God.

I love my mother deeply. Not in spite of her brokenness, but with a deeper tenderness because of it. I know now that broken stories are often the very places where God's redemption shines brightest. My prayer is that one day she will surrender fully to the Lord—the only One who can heal the losses of her childhood, restore the years grief tried to steal, and tell her who she has always been beneath the sorrow.

Her story may have begun with loneliness, but I do not believe loneliness gets the final word.

Because God does not abandon the

forgotten.

Even the little girl who once whispered into the dark, "Mama, where are you?" was never unseen. She was known. She was carried. She was loved by the One who never leaves.

And maybe that is where my family's redemption begins: not with perfection, not with answers, but with the hope that even our most shattered beginnings can still be rewritten by the Hand of God.

CHAPTER 2

THE PRIDE FAMILY—- "GENERATIONAL PAIN ENDS WHEN TRUTH BEGINS."

Pride goes before destruction, and a haughty spirit before a fall." Proverbs 16:18

I grew up mostly knowing my mother's side of the family, though even "knowing" may be too generous a word. We were connected by blood, but not always by closeness. Family existed more as scattered branches than as one strong tree. My mother kept her circle small, visiting only certain relatives, speaking of others rarely or with caution. Years passed before she finally took us to see her grandmother.

We did not have family reunions. There were no large gatherings filled with laughter and storytelling, no sense of shared inheritance strong enough to pull everyone back together. Thanksgiving and Christmas came the closest, and even then, it was usually just my mother's sisters and their children gathered in the same room, carrying old habits and unspoken tensions like extra guests at the table.

My oldest aunt carried herself as if she had risen above everyone else. She could be pleasant in flashes, even fun when the mood suited her, but there was a cold superiority underneath it. She praised my sister often—her grades, her ambition, her college path—and though maybe she did not realize the weight of her favoritism, my brother and I felt it. We were there, but not fully seen. She seemed to hold my sister up as a model for her own twin daughters, as if one child's shine could be used to brighten another's future. Life, of course, had its own plans. I still think of those girls sometimes and hope they found peace on whatever roads they took.

My mother's youngest sister was different. She had been shaped more visibly by survival. After their mother died, life in the projects left its mark on her. She was vibrant, loud, rough around the edges, drawn to men and places that reflected the hardness she had learned to live inside. There was love in her, but it was often buried under the instincts of self-protection. She had children of her own, and like so many in my family, she was doing her best while carrying wounds that had never truly been healed.

Not every memory was heavy.

One of the brightest people in that family line was my mother's great aunt. She was warmth in human form. When we visited her, she welcomed us with a smile that seemed to open the whole house. There was always food, always affection, always a softness in the way she spoke. She kissed cheeks, asked questions, made you feel that your presence mattered. In a family where emotional distance often felt normal, she stood out to me as proof that love could survive even in broken soil.

There was also my mother's aunt, her mother's sister, who had three daughters of her own. Each seemed to carry her own temperament, her own way of moving through the family's currents of silence and strain. One was quiet, one energetic, one removed. The youngest rarely came around, kept away by some wound between her and her mother that I only understood in pieces. In my family, estrangement was rarely announced. It just settled in and stayed.

It was not until high school that I met more of my mother's extended family—other aunts, uncles, great-aunts, great-uncles. Some seemed kind enough, but even then I could sense it: an undercurrent running through the family like something inherited. Pride. Bitterness.

Hardness. A meanness that surfaced in sharp words, in emotional distance, in how easily people seemed to wound one another and keep moving.

One great-aunt of mine was known for that hardness. She taught first grade at Washington School in Titusville, and I sat in her classroom as a child. I still remember the ruler in her hand and the sting of it against my skin when I whispered. There was no gentleness in her correction, no warmth in the way she carried authority. Children feared her. I did too.

As I grew older, my mother shared more of the family history with me. She told me that some of this coldness went back generations—that her grandmother's father had been a harsh and possibly abusive man, cruel to his wife, sowing pain that outlived him. Whatever happened in that house did not stay there. It spread through the family line, showing up as pride, unforgiveness, emotional distance, and the kind of meanness that becomes so normal people stop questioning it.

The more I looked, the more clearly I could see it.

This was a family divided against itself. Not always in dramatic ways, but in quieter, more enduring ones. There were no deep bonds holding everyone together, no culture of repair, no steady practice of forgiveness. People stayed in their own corners, protecting their own hurts, nursing old wounds until those wounds became part of their identity. Households survived side by side, but healing rarely crossed the threshold.

Shame lived there. So did silence. So did pride.

And yet, even as a child, something in me resisted the idea that this had to be the end of the story.

As I grew in faith, I began to understand that generational brokenness may be inherited, but it does not have to be perpetuated. The patterns handed down to me were real, but they were not sovereign. Jesus interrupts what families normalize. He confronts what generations excuse. He breaks what people assume can never change.

Where pride has ruled, He teaches humility.

Where bitterness has hardened hearts, He teaches forgiveness.

Where shame has hidden in the bloodline, He covers with grace.

I was born into a family marked by division, but I refuse to make division my inheritance. I do not want to pass down silence, coldness, or unresolved pain to the generations after me. I want my children to know something holier than survival. I want them to know love that repairs, truth that heals, and grace that breaks cycles.

The family line I came from may have been marked by pride.

But in Christ, the cycle stops with me.

CHAPTER 3

MOMMY DEAREST - "RAISED BY SURVIVAL, NOT SOFTNESS."

"He heals the brokenhearted and binds up their wounds." Psalms 147:3 NIV

Some of my earliest memories are rooted in the Titusville projects of Birmingham, Alabama. I was four years old, living with my mother, my brother, and my sister in a world that felt small and hard and normal all at once. As children, we accepted whatever life gave us because we had nothing else to compare it to. The projects were simply where we lived. Hardship was simply how life worked.

My mother worked, so we learned early how to fend for ourselves in ways children should not have to. We walked to school. We followed routines because there was no other choice. On Sundays, our aunt took us to Porter Chapel C.M.E. Church in Bessemer. My mother did not go with us then. She was trying to survive in the only ways she knew, and survival took so much out of her that there was often little left over.

Even as a child, I understood that my mother was carrying something heavy. I just did not know yet how much that heaviness would spill into us.

One of the first memories burned into me is not a birthday or a holiday, but violence.

I remember hearing shouting downstairs and creeping toward the noise to see what was happening. What I saw there was shocking.

There was blood on the floor. My mother had stabbed her boyfriend. Soon the house filled with sirens, flashing lights, voices, uniforms, and confusion. Police and paramedics moved through our home while my siblings and I stood inside the chaos of an adult world we could not understand.

That night scarred me.

It taught me, long before I had language for it, that love could turn dangerous without warning. That home was not always safe. That what should comfort you could also wound you.

When that relationship ended, another man entered our lives, and with him came another move—this time to a house in Woodlawn. To a child, a new house can feel like a promise. I wanted to believe this was a fresh start, that stability might finally take root. But brokenness travels easily when no one knows how to confront it.

While my mother and her boyfriend worked, my sister often watched my brother and I. Rules existed, but they were fragile. Friends came over when they were not supposed to. Boundaries blurred. We played childish games without understanding how quickly childhood innocence can be crossed. One day, we found a stack of pornographic tapes belonging to my mother's boyfriend. My sister put one into the VCR, and we watched things no children should ever see.

That moment did not stand alone. It became part of a larger pattern in my life—a pattern of being exposed too early, seeing too much, carrying things a child's mind and body were never meant to hold.

Violence followed us to Woodlawn too.

I vividly remember another fight, another eruption, another scene that made me feel powerless inside my own home. My mother and her boyfriend were attacking one another, and I watched her grab a large butcher knife and stab him just as she had done before. He ran. There was blood again. There were police again. And this time, my mother was taken away in handcuffs.

My siblings and I were sent to stay with our aunt until she got out of jail.

Even now, that sentence sits heavily in me. Children should not have to carry those kinds of memories. But we did. We carried them because there was no one else to carry them for us.

That relationship ended too, and in time another man came into the picture—a stepfather this time. He had a son, and for a little while it felt like maybe we were stepping into something closer to family. We went to church together. There was structure, at least for a season. I remember the feeling of wanting it to last.

But instability had become its own kind of inheritance.

Eventually dysfunction surfaced again. My brother found a gun in the house and brought it to school. He was expelled, and our lives shifted once more, uprooted and moved to Pinson as though constant disruption were just another ordinary part of childhood.

By middle school, rebellion had begun to bloom in me too. I snuck out. I searched for affection in foolish places. I got caught sleeping in a shed with a boy I liked, and though punishment followed, what I was really doing was looking for something I could not name. Safety. Love. Belonging. Relief. I was reaching for comfort with the clumsy hands of a wounded girl.

By high school, we were living in Trussville, and for the first time I found something that made me feel alive in a clean and honest way: track and field.

Running gave me freedom. It gave me discipline. It gave me a place where my body could do something other than carry fear. On the track, I felt purposeful. On the team, I felt like I belonged to something bigger than the turmoil at home. It was one of the few places in my early life where I felt joy without confusion attached to it.

But that too was interrupted.

When my mother's marriage fell apart and financial pressure closed in around us, I became one of the people she leaned on. I wasn't allowed to chase my athletic dreams, I was forced to get a job and help with bills. I handed over money while still barely old enough to understand the cost of growing up too soon. Little by little, my youth slipped away under the weight of adult responsibilities.

My mother was pursuing her dream of interior design, trying to build a future out of talent and determination, but the bills kept piling up. Food became scarce. The house went into foreclosure. And then came the moment that carved another wound into me: she told my brother and I that we would have to "get out" and find somewhere else to live.

I was barely twenty years old.

Not ready. Not stable. Not secure.

I remember reaching out to relatives on my mother's side, hoping someone would open a door. Surely family would make room. Surely blood would mean something in a moment like this. But one by one, the answers came back as some version of no. Even my aunt, the one closest to my mother, did not take me in, though her own children were already gone.

That rejection cut deep. It confirmed a fear I had carried for years: that family could be near and still not be there for you.

So I did what I had done my whole life. I survived.

At first, a friend let me stay on her couch. Then, in time, I found refuge at my grandmother's house—my father's mother. And there, after years of absence, I saw my father again for the first time since I was three years old.

That reunion was not simple. It came with questions too old to ignore and wounds too deep to dismiss. I did not know how to approach a man who had been a stranger for most of my life. I did not know what to do with the anger, the distance, the longing, or the grief. But looking back, I can see that even this was a turning point. Survival had carried me to a place where my past and my future could finally stand in the same room.

When I think about my childhood now, I do not think of it only as a string of tragedies. I think of it as a landscape marked by violence, instability, betrayal, and loss—but also by the quiet, relentless mercy of God.

I did not always recognize Him then. I did not know how to name His presence. But He was there.

He was there in every door that opened just enough to keep me from falling all the way through.

He was there in every moment I should have been destroyed but wasn't.

He was there in the hidden work of preserving a heart that still, somehow, kept hoping.

Faith did not come to me all at once. It came in fragments, just as so much else in my life had. Through pain. Through failure. Through the ache of having nowhere left to turn.

What I thought was only survival was, in truth, the beginning of redemption.

Because God was not just keeping me alive.

He was carrying me toward Himself.

CHAPTER 4

SISTER ACT—- "WHEN LOVE AND PAIN WEAR THE SAME FACE."

""If anyone causes one of these little ones—those who believe in me—to stumble, it would be better for them if a large millstone were hung around their neck and they were thrown into the sea."

Mark 9:42 NIV

Growing up with my sister was like trying to love someone who lived in two different worlds.

She was four years older than me, and though we shared the same mother, we did not share the same father—or the same emotional language. There were moments when she was warm, playful, and full of life. In those moments, I felt like I had the sister I always wanted. I held onto those glimpses of her like something rare and fragile.

But just as often, she was distant. Sharp. Unpredictable.

I never knew which version of her I would get.

She spent a lot of time away from home, staying with her dad or other relatives, so the moments we shared were scattered. But a couple of memories remain etched into my mind, as if time slowed down just to make sure I would never forget it.

I was still a child—too young to understand anger the way she carried it. Our mom was at work. Something small turned into something big, the way it often did in our house. Voices raised. Tension thickened. And suddenly, we were running.

She chased us.

My brother first. She pinned him down, her hands around his neck. I remember the panic rising in me, something primal, something urgent. I didn't think—I just reacted. I kicked her with everything I had, pulling her off him.

And then I ran.

I thought I could escape into the bathroom. I thought a door could protect me.

But she followed.

The moment replays in my mind in slow motion. The door bursts open. Her hands are on me before I can move. Fingers tight around my throat. Pressure. Tightening.

The room starts to blur.

I remember the way her eyes looked—cold, distant, almost as if she wasn't fully there. That frightened me more than the choking itself. It felt like something had taken over her, something I could not fight.

For a moment, I thought I was going to die.

And then, somehow, it stopped.

I lived. But something in me changed.

That moment planted a fear deep inside me—not just of her, but of closeness itself. It taught me that even people who are supposed to love you can hurt you in ways that leave no visible scars.

But that wasn't the only wound.

There are other memories—darker ones, ones I wish I didn't carry. She was the first person who introduced me to something I should have never known as a child. The first time was in the Titusville projects, when I was in kindergarten. The second was in our home in Woodlawn, while I was still in elementary school. Both times, she physically forced me to perform acts on her that I didn't understand. In those vile, cringy moments that seemed like an eternity, a level of self worth was lost and a measure of trust was shattered. Those experiences didn't just confuse me...both times, every morsel of innocence inside me broke.

Those experiences shaped how I saw myself.

How I saw love.

How I understood my body.

And yet, even in all of that, my feelings toward my sister were never simple.

I admired her.

I watched her excel in school, in sports, in life. She made straight A's. She played volleyball and basketball with a confidence I didn't have. She seemed to move through the world with purpose, while I felt like I was just trying to keep up.

I wanted to be like her—at least the parts of her that shined.

I dreamed of us being close. The kind of sisters who told each other everything, who defended each other, who laughed more than they hurt each other. But that kind of relationship never came.

Instead, what remained was something more complicated.

Love tangled with pain.

Admiration mixed with fear.

Longing wrapped in silence.

My sister was my blood.

But she was also my first wound.

CHAPTER 5

UNWANTED —-"OFFERING MY HEART TO THOSE WHO DIDN'T DESERVE IT."

"Do not be afraid; you will not be put to shame. Do not fear disgrace; you will not be humiliated. You will forget the shame of your youth and remember no more the reproach of your widowhood."

Isaiah 54:4 NIV

Being in high school was sometimes fun… and other times not so much.

I remember watching how certain guys were drawn to certain girls—the ones they considered pretty. The girls who seemed to shine without trying. The ones who got attention just by walking into a room. Some of them even gained popularity simply because of how they looked.

And I noticed.

I liked some of those same guys. But somewhere deep down, I believed they would never like me back.

Not because they knew me.

But because of how I saw myself.

One day, I stood in the girls' bathroom, staring at my reflection in the mirror. I don't remember anyone else being in there. It was just me… and my thoughts.

And out loud, I said it.

"You are ugly."

"No guy wants to be with you."

The words didn't just come from my mouth—they came from a place that had already started forming inside of me.

And as I stood there, I cried.

That moment may have seemed small to anyone else... but for me, it was the beginning of something deeper. That was when low self-esteem took root in my heart—and it didn't stay small.

It grew.

From that point on, I never really saw myself as a pretty girl. No matter what anyone else said—or didn't say—I had already decided what I believed about myself.

And that belief followed me.

It shaped how I saw love.

How I accepted attention.

How I allowed people to treat me.

Because when you don't believe you're worthy... you start accepting anything that feels close to being chosen.

I was sixteen when I first thought I had found love.

We had just moved to Center Point, Alabama. Everything felt new—unfamiliar, unsettled. And then I met him at a park near our house. He was older, confident, easy to talk to. I didn't know the kind of life he lived. I didn't know the weight of the choices he had already made.

All I knew was how he made me feel.

Seen.

Wanted.

Important.

And so I let him in.

Too far. Too fast.

One day, while my mom was at work, I invited him over. That was the day I lost my virginity—not out of understanding, not out of readiness, but out of longing.

Not long after, we moved back to Trussville. But he followed. He came into our home when my mom wasn't there, and for a while, it felt like I had something that belonged to me.

Until the day it all came crashing down.

My mom came home early. I remember the panic, the sound of him running out the door, the anger that followed. She stormed into my room, her words cutting deeper than anything else.

That moment didn't just expose my actions—it exposed how broken things already were.

I ran away that night.

For nearly a week, I stayed gone, clinging to the idea that I had found something real. But eventually, reality pulled me back. I returned home, carrying both shame and confusion, not fully understanding what I had stepped into.

That relationship ended.

But the pattern didn't.

As I grew older, relationships became the place where I searched for what I had been missing all along—love, security, identity. But instead, I often found pain.

I remember in 2008, I began to pray.

Not casually—but with hope.

I asked God for a man of God. I believed He would send someone different. Someone right.

Around that time, I was attending Walking on Water Christian Church in Center Point, Alabama. I joined the youth choir, trying to stay connected to something deeper than what I had been living.

And that's where I saw him.

He stood out immediately—handsome, confident, and gifted. He could sing, and there was something about him that caught my attention.

I remember thinking, *He looks like he would be a good boyfriend.*

I didn't know him yet. I hadn't seen his heart. But I had already started imagining what he could be.

Eventually, we began a relationship. We went to the same church. We attended Jefferson State Community College together. It felt aligned—like maybe this was the answer to the prayer I had prayed.

But what I thought was answered prayer became one of my deepest heartbreaks.

One evening in the fall of 2009, I was walking to my car on campus. The day was winding down, and everything felt still.

Until I saw him.

He was standing across the street with another girl—hugging her, kissing her—like I didn't exist.

Something inside me broke instantly.

I walked over to him, barely holding myself together. He looked at me, then led me into a nearby building.

And with a calmness that felt almost detached, he said, "Let's just be friends."

Then he walked back outside to her.

In that moment, my heart didn't just hurt—it collapsed.

I stood there crying, trying to process what had just happened. That was the first time I had ever been rejected like that by someone I believed loved me.

But heartbreak has a way of pulling you back into what hurts you.

In 2010, he came back.

He said he wanted to try again—to fix what was broken. And I let him. I believed things would be different.

They weren't.

That relationship lasted five years.

There were moments that felt like love—but they were overshadowed by manipulation, control, and violence. There were nights I feared for my life. Nights I felt physically hurt, emotionally drained, spiritually empty.

And still… I stayed.

Not because I didn't see the damage.

But because I didn't yet see my worth.

In 2012, everything shifted again.

I found out I was pregnant.

It was my first pregnancy, and fear immediately took hold of me. I had heard all my life that abortion was a sin—that God wouldn't forgive it. That belief sat heavy in my spirit.

But at the same time, I knew something else just as clearly:

I wasn't ready.

Our lives were unstable. We didn't have a solid home. No real foundation. And deep down, I knew I didn't want to bring a child into the chaos I was living in.

And even harder to admit…

I didn't want a child by him.

When I told him, he was happy.

But I wasn't.

I told him the truth. That we weren't ready. That our relationship wasn't healthy. That this wasn't the life I wanted to bring a child into.

And I made the decision to have an abortion.

When I went to the clinic, there were people standing outside—holding signs, shouting, condemning. Every time I went, they were there. Their voices loud with judgment.

But I walked past them anyway.

Inside, I chose the abortion pill.

That weekend, while staying at my sister's house, I took it. The process happened that same day.

And afterward, I felt relief.

Not because it was easy. Not because it didn't matter.

But because I knew I had stepped away from something that would have tied me permanently to a situation that was already breaking me.

At the time, I didn't fully understand the weight of that decision.

I didn't yet understand God's grace the way I do now.

I was making decisions from a place of pain, fear, and survival.

And still—God never left me.

The relationship continued, growing darker with time.

There were nights filled with anger, control, and fear. Nights where things escalated beyond what I thought I could survive.

The night he pushed me out of a moving car should have been the end.

I hit the ground, shaken and breathless—but alive.

And then God intervened.

A woman driving behind us stopped. She pulled me to safety, stood between me and danger, and made sure I got home.

I didn't know her.

But I knew she was sent.

Still, leaving wasn't easy.

It took another voice—another woman, older and wiser—to help me see clearly. She listened without judgment. She spoke truth without fear. And she gave me the courage I didn't have on my own.

And finally, at the end of 2013...

I left.

I walked away.

And I lived.

But even after that, I wasn't whole.

In 2016, I entered another relationship—lighter, less intense, but still not rooted in anything real. I wanted more than he did. And when he made that clear, I found myself back in a familiar place...

Feeling unwanted.

But something had shifted.

God was drawing me closer.

Through His Word. Through Bible study. Through quiet moments where truth began to rise above emotion.

I started to see what I hadn't seen before.

That my search for love in people…

was really a deeper search for God.

And for the first time, I began to let Him fill the spaces I had been trying to fill with everything else.

Because what I once called rejection… was actually redirection.

CHAPTER 6

INTRO TO BABYLON— -"FREEDOM WITHOUT GOD IS STILL BONDAGE."

"Even if you have been banished to the most distant land under the heavens, from there the Lord your God will gather you and bring you back."

Deuteronomy 30:4 NIV

When I left home for college, I carried more than clothes and books with me. I carried a quiet determination—a need to prove that I could build something different from what I came from.

I didn't know exactly what my future looked like, but I knew I couldn't stay where I had been.

In 2009, I enrolled at Jefferson State Community College. I thought this was my way forward. But that first attempt ended in failure. I didn't have the discipline yet. I didn't have the foundation. And when I fell, it felt like confirmation of every doubt I had ever carried about myself.

Still, something in me refused to give up.

I was accepted into The Art Institute, but I couldn't shake the feeling that something wasn't right. At the time, I didn't have the language for it, but now I know—it was God. Even before I fully knew Him, He was guiding me.

I tried the military next. Another closed door.

Asthma. Failed tests. Rejection again.

By the time I reached 2010, I was tired—but I wasn't finished.

At twenty-one, I enrolled at Lawson State Community College. Somehow, financial aid came through again, even though it had been taken from me before. That moment felt like grace, even if I didn't fully understand it yet.

But school was only one part of the battle.

After my mother put me out, I had nowhere stable to go. I moved from place to place—friends' homes, temporary spaces, anywhere that would take me. Stability was something I had to piece together day by day.

Eventually, I found some grounding at my grandmother's house. It wasn't perfect, but it was enough.

In 2011, I started working at Lowe's while continuing school. Then came another obstacle—my car broke down. Repairs cost more than I could afford. I reached out for help, hoping someone would step in. But instead, I was met with rejection.

That moment taught me something painful but necessary: people are not always dependable.

So I adjusted.

Without a car, I rode the bus. Early mornings. Dark streets. Long rides across the city. Every day required effort just to get where I needed to go. And though I didn't say it out loud then, I know now that God was protecting me through all of it.

Eventually, I saved enough to buy a used car. It wasn't fancy, but it was mine. Another step forward.

In 2012, I transferred to Jacksonville State University. I stayed focused. I didn't get caught up in the party scene the way others did. I had a goal, and I held onto it.

By December 2015, I graduated.

In March 2016, I started working full-time at St. Vincent's. I moved into my own apartment downtown. For the first time, I felt like I had made it somewhere. Like I had built something out of all the instability behind me.

But success didn't mean wholeness.

Even in that season, I found myself drifting. Nights out. Drinking. Risky choices. Living in ways that could have ended badly more than once.

Looking back, I realize I was still searching—just in the wrong places.

That season was my Babylon.

A place where I was free, but not grounded.

Independent, but not whole.

Living, but not fully alive.

And yet, even there, God was with me.

I didn't recognize Him at the time, but He was there in every protection, every open door, every moment I should have lost everything—but didn't.

I thought I was just surviving.

But God was positioning me.

CHAPTER 7

A CRY FOR HELP – "MEETING GOD IN THE VALLEY "

"The righteous cry out, and the Lord hears them; He delivers them from all their troubles." Psalm 34:17

There was a night I will never forget.

I sat on the edge of my bed, knees pulled into my chest, my room wrapped in a silence that felt heavier than noise. Everything inside me felt like it was collapsing at once—failure, shame, loneliness—all pressing in until I could barely breathe under the weight of it.

I had just lost my financial aid at Jefferson State Community College. Not because I wasn't capable, but because fear had paralyzed me. I couldn't stand in front of a class and speak. I chose silence, and that silence cost me more than a grade—it cost me progress, confidence, and the fragile belief that I was moving forward.

That night, the darkness in my room matched the darkness in my thoughts.

A voice—quiet, but persistent—began whispering something dangerous: Maybe your life doesn't matter. Maybe it would be easier if you weren't here at all.

I didn't know how to fight those thoughts. I didn't have the words, the strength, or the understanding. But something deep inside me—something I now know was God—rose up anyway.

And I cried out.

Not politely. Not perfectly.

Desperately.

"God, I need You! God, I need You!"

I said it over and over again, tears streaming down my face, my voice breaking under the weight of everything I had been carrying. I wasn't praying from knowledge. I wasn't praying from faith.

I was praying from emptiness.

And then I fell asleep.

Looking back, I know that was the moment everything began to change. Not overnight. Not instantly. But something shifted. That cry did not fall into silence the way my mother's childhood prayers had.

God heard me.

And from that moment on, I began to search for Him.

I didn't know what I was looking for exactly, but I knew I couldn't keep living the way I had been. I started going to church more consistently. I didn't understand everything, but I knew one thing clearly: if there was a way out of the pit I was in, it had to be through God.

When probation forced me to sit out a semester, I didn't quit. I transferred to Lawson State and kept moving forward. But even as I progressed externally, something inside me remained unsettled.

I had been in church all my life—on and off—but it never felt like enough.

Between the ages of five and twenty-eight, I had walked through the doors of at least ten different churches. And every time, something inside me whispered the same thing:

There has to be more than this.

That hunger wouldn't let me rest.

While working at Lowe's, I began slipping away during my lunch breaks to a nearby bookstore. That's where I found a copy of The Message Bible. When I opened it, something shifted. The words felt alive—like they were reaching for me, speaking directly into places I didn't even know how to express.

Later, I found the NIV, and for the first time, I could follow along without feeling lost in language I didn't understand.

I wanted to know God—not just hear about Him.

I even signed up for an Old Testament class, hoping knowledge would bring clarity. But still, it felt like I was reaching for something just beyond my grasp.

Even after transferring to Jacksonville State University, I kept searching. I bought a parallel Bible, reading it late into the night, trying to make sense of what I felt stirring inside me.

I didn't have all the answers.

But I had a hunger that wouldn't go away.

And that hunger was leading me somewhere.

CHAPTER 8

THE TRUTH HURTS - "GOD SHOWED ME ME—AND IT CHANGED EVERYTHING."

"For the word of God is alive and active, sharper than any double-edged sword..." Hebrews 4:12

I used to think I was a good person.

Not perfect—but good enough. I didn't see myself as someone who had done serious wrong. I believed I treated people fairly. I believed my intentions counted for something.

But the Word of God has a way of cutting through what we believe about ourselves and revealing what's actually there.

And when I began to truly listen—not casually, not selectively, but honestly—the truth came for me.

And it hurt.

It didn't just challenge me—it exposed me.

I realized that my greatest betrayal wasn't toward other people. It was toward God. I had lived my life according to my own understanding, following my own desires, trusting my own judgment. I thought I was independent, strong, in control.

But in reality, I was disconnected.

I had been given life by my Creator, and I had chosen to live as though I didn't need Him.

That realization shook me.

And then God began to take me deeper.

He didn't just show me my present—He walked me back through my past.

I saw my childhood differently. I saw the rebellion that had been in me from an early age—the ways I had resisted my mother's guidance, pushed boundaries, and chosen my own way even when it led to harm.

I saw my relationship with my sister—not just how I had been hurt, but how I had hurt her too. The pride that kept me from attending her wedding. The distance I created. The ways I had failed to love her well.

I saw my relationships clearly for the first time.

The five-year relationship I had labeled as purely abusive—God showed me the truth. Yes, I had been hurt. But I wasn't blameless. My jealousy, my pride, my reactions—they had all contributed to the destruction.

That truth was hard to swallow.

After that relationship ended, I ran into another one without healing. A man and his mother opened their home to me when I had nowhere else to go. They showed me kindness, stability—and I still left in a way that caused harm.

And then came the hardest truth of all.

The man God brought into my life—the one who would become my husband. A man who loved me faithfully, who covered me with grace, who gave me something I had never truly experienced before.

And still… I rebelled.

I was unfaithful—not just physically, but in

my heart. I resisted what God was trying to build. I dishonored something sacred.

That truth broke me.

By 2018, I couldn't carry the weight of who I had been anymore.

I fell to my knees—not out of obligation, but because I had nowhere else to go. Pride shattered. Tears came freely. Repentance was no longer a concept—it was survival.

God showed me everything.

Pride.

Rebellion.

Selfishness.

Disobedience.

It wasn't condemnation—it was exposure. And in that exposure, there was an invitation:

Let Me change you.

And so I began the process.

Slow. Painful. Necessary.

God wasn't just correcting my behavior—He was transforming my heart.

And for the first time, I stopped running from the truth.

I let it do its work.

CHAPTER 9

A TIME TO HEAL- "HEALING BEGAN WHERE PRIDE ENDED."

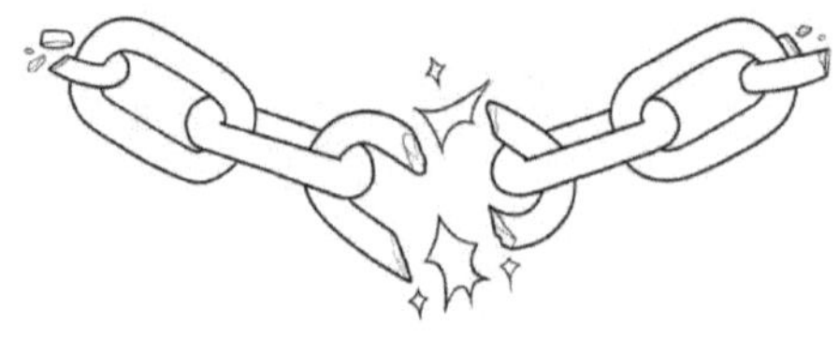

"a time to kill and a time to heal, a time to tear down and a time to build," -Ecclesiastes 3:3 NIV

It started in March 2017, though I didn't realize at the time how significant it would become.

I was on a road trip with my mom, headed to

South Carolina. It was supposed to be a simple getaway. But God had something else planned.

My phone rang.

It was the man who had begun to play a pivotal role in my spiritual journey—the one who would later become my husband. His voice was calm, steady, but what he said carried weight.

He began talking about the parable in John's Gospel chapter 4 of the woman at the well. But not in the way I had heard it before. He spoke about "husbands" not just as relationships, but as spiritual leadership—about how the woman had been under multiple influences, multiple coverings.

And then he said something that pierced straight through me:

"Somebody needs to forgive someone."

My chest tightened.

I knew he was talking to me.

Not because he knew my story—but because God did.

In that moment, I realized I had been carrying things I had never fully released. Hurt. Resentment. Old wounds that had quietly shaped how I saw people, how I loved, how I trusted.

If I wanted freedom, I had to let them go.

That weekend, I began making calls.

Each one felt heavier than the last.

The first was to an ex-boyfriend. My voice trembled as I spoke, but I didn't hold back.

"I've given my life to God," I told him. "And I need to apologize. For how I hurt you. For how I left. You didn't deserve that."

There was silence. Then a shift. Something softened between us.

I made another call. Then another.

Each conversation felt like tearing down a

wall I had built to protect myself. Walls made of pride, fear, and self-justification.

But the hardest call... was to my father.

I hadn't said much to him over the years. His absence had left questions, wounds, and a quiet ache I didn't always acknowledge.

When I called him, my voice felt small.

"Daddy... I forgive you."

The words surprised even me.

I didn't say them because everything was resolved. I said them because I finally understood something: he was human. Broken in his own ways. Shaped by his own pain.

That didn't excuse what was missing.

But it freed me from carrying it.

The journey didn't end there.

In 2018, God took me deeper.

I sat across from my sister in a restaurant, knowing this conversation mattered. She didn't hold back. She told me how I had hurt her—missing her wedding, not showing up for her when it mattered, disrespecting her home.

Every word landed.

And everything in me wanted to defend myself.

But God told me to listen.

So I did.

When she finished, I looked at her through tears and said the only thing that mattered:

"I'm sorry. For all of it. Please forgive me."

And she did.

In that moment, once again, something broke—not between us, but inside me.

Chains I didn't even realize I was carrying fell off.

Forgiveness didn't erase the past.

But it freed me from it.

I began to understand that healing doesn't come from being right—it comes from being honest. From laying everything down before God and letting Him rebuild what pride once held together.

For years, I thought I was "not that bad."

But truth showed me otherwise.

And grace met me there anyway.

Forgiveness became more than something I gave others—it became something God gave me.

And in that exchange, I found freedom.

CHAPTER 10

SAVE THE LAST DANCE "GOD WAS LEADING LONG BEFORE I SURRENDERED."

"In their hearts humans plan their course, but the Lord establishes their steps." Proverbs 16:9 NIV

There are moments in life that seem ordinary when they happen—but later, you realize heaven was moving the entire time.

February 6, 2016 was one of those moments.

My mother and I went to Olivia's Bar & Lounge in downtown Birmingham to celebrate a new beginning—my first full-time job. I remember sitting there, taking it all in. The music. The lights. The feeling that maybe, finally, my life was coming together.

And then he walked up to me.

He didn't say much. He simply extended his hand.

I looked at him, confused. I didn't dance in front of people. I didn't like attention. Fear had always kept me small, always whispered that I was safer staying in the background.

But he didn't move his hand.

He waited.

And something in me—something quiet but undeniable—said yes.

So I gave him my hand.

On that dance floor, something shifted. We laughed, moved, and for a moment, everything else faded away. It felt like we were the only two people in the room. I followed his lead without overthinking, without fear, without the weight I usually carried.

And then he said it.

"I'm gonna marry you."

I laughed. How could a man say something like that after just meeting me? But something about him stayed with me. Something deeper than attraction. Something I couldn't explain.

That same night, after the music faded, he began talking about something I wasn't expecting—God.

Not the kind of conversation I had heard growing up in church. This was different. There was depth. There was clarity. There was conviction.

I didn't fully understand it then, but I felt it.

A seed was planted.

The next day, I saw him again.

A red car with a beige top pulled up, and I knew it was him before I even saw his face. My heart reacted before my mind could catch up.

But when I saw another woman near him, I pulled back just as quickly.

That's over, I told myself.

And just like that, I moved on. Or at least, I thought I did.

At that point in my life, everything looked like it was finally coming together. I had my own place, my own job, my own independence. I was going to church, spending time with friends, living the life I thought I wanted.

But deep down, something was still missing.

When my mom invited me to Bible study at the radio station, I went out of curiosity. What

I heard there challenged everything I thought I knew about God. The Word came alive in a way I had never experienced before.

Still, I wasn't fully surrendered.

I lived in two worlds.

One foot in truth.

One foot in distraction.

One night I was in the Word. The next, I was out dancing, drinking, chasing temporary joy.

I was searching—but I hadn't committed.

But God is patient.

Even when we resist Him, He continues to draw us.

By March 2017, something began to shift. What started as curiosity became connection. What I once questioned, I began to embrace.

And through it all, he was still there.

Anthony.

The man I had once dismissed.

The man who carried truth in a way I couldn't ignore.

As we spent more time together, I began to see something different. Something steady. Something real. Not just in him—but in what God was doing through him.

Then came the test.

One night on March 17, 2018 in Savannah, Georgia, another woman approached him and asked to dance. Everything in me reacted. Old feelings rose up—jealousy, insecurity, pride.

I had a choice.

React… or trust.

For the first time in my life, I chose differently.

I chose love.

It wasn't easy. It didn't feel natural. But it was the first moment I realized I was no longer the same person I used to be.

God was changing me.

Then came the biggest step of all.

In 2020, life shifted again. Rising rent forced a decision I didn't want to make. Anthony asked me to move to Anniston—to live with him and his family.

Everything in me resisted.

I liked my independence. My space. My control.

But deep down, I heard something stronger than fear:

Trust Me.

So I did.

I stepped out of what was comfortable and into what was uncertain—but ordained.

And just a few months later, everything changed again.

In December 2020, I found out I was pregnant.

Looking back, I see what I couldn't see then.

God was never absent.

Not in the lounge.

Not on the dance floor.

Not in the confusion.

He was leading the entire time.

This wasn't just a love story between two people.

It was a redemption story between a daughter and her Father.

Because I wasn't just learning how to love a man.

I was learning how to surrender to God.

That night in 2016, I thought I was just dancing.

But now I understand—

God was leading every step.

And all along…

He was saving the last dance for redemption.

CHAPTER 11

A NEW BEGINNING—- "WHAT I THOUGHT I LOST, GOD RESTORED."

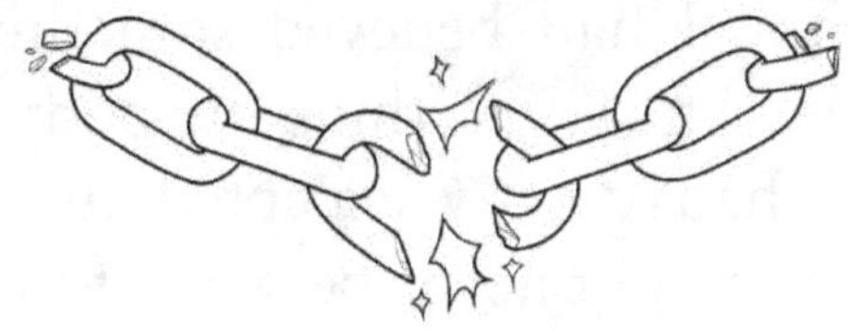

"Therefore, if anyone is in Christ, the new creation has come: The old has gone, the new is here!"

2 Corinthians 5:17 NIV

I still remember the moment everything changed.

It was December 2020, and I was staring at something I never thought I would see—a positive pregnancy test.

I didn't just feel surprised.

I felt undone.

For years, I had believed something in me was broken. After everything my body had gone through, I had quietly accepted the idea that motherhood might never be part of my story.

But God had already decided otherwise.

As I sat there, holding that reality in my hands, I felt caught between fear and wonder.

How could this be?

And yet, life was already growing inside of me—proof that what I thought was impossible had already begun.

In August 2021, I gave birth to my first

daughter.

Holding her in my arms felt like holding a miracle.

But even in that joy, there was a battle.

The days after her birth were heavy. Emotions I didn't fully understand tried to pull me under. Thoughts that didn't belong to me tried to take root.

But I refused to surrender to them.

I fought—not just for myself, but for her.

Every day, I chose to show up. To care for her. To love her. To protect her. Even when I felt overwhelmed. Even when I didn't feel strong.

And through it all, God carried me.

At the same time, God was building something bigger than I could see.

Through Bible studies on Clubhouse, lives were being changed. Truth was spreading.

People were being awakened. What started as simple conversations became a spiritual family—one built on the Word of God.

We became part of that family.

Spirit and Truth.

And while I was learning how to be a mother, I was also being built spiritually. Surrounded by people who loved God and loved truth.

Then God did it again.

In 2022, I conceived another child.

Another miracle.

Another daughter.

And then again in 2024.

Three daughters.

Three miracles.

All through one fallopian tube.

Because years earlier, I had been told

something that tried to define my future.

In the summer of 2015, I had an ectopic pregnancy. Emergency surgery. Fear. Loss. And when I woke up, I was told that one of my fallopian tubes had been removed. The left fallopian tube.

In that moment, I believed motherhood might be out of reach.

But God had the final word.

What doctors saw as limitation, God used as evidence of His power.

Through what remained, He gave me more than I ever imagined.

My first birth was shaped by fear. I listened to voices that told me what I couldn't handle.

But the second time, I chose differently.

I chose faith.

At a birthing center, surrounded by peace instead of pressure, I gave birth naturally. No medication. No fear. Just trust.

The Word of God filled the room. Worship replaced anxiety. And my body did exactly what God designed it to do.

It was freeing.

It was powerful.

It was proof.

By the time my third daughter came, I had fully surrendered. Labor came quickly, unexpectedly—and before I could even process it, she was in my arms.

Another reminder.

God knows exactly what He's doing.

When I look back over my life now, I don't just see moments—I see a pattern.

A pattern of grace.

A woman who once believed she was broken… now holding three living miracles.

A heart once filled with fear… now walking in faith.

A life once searching for purpose… now living in it.

God didn't just give me children.

He restored me.

He healed places I didn't even know were wounded. He replaced fear with trust, doubt with faith, emptiness with abundance.

And now I understand something I didn't before:

I was never disqualified.

I was being prepared.

Today, I stand in gratitude.

Not because my life is perfect—but because it is redeemed.

Every scar. Every mistake. Every broken place—it all led me here. To a place where I can finally see that God has been writing my story all along.

And if there is one thing I know for sure, it's this:

He is not finished with me yet.

Because the same God who brought life where I thought there was none...

Is the same God who will continue to bring beauty from every broken place.

CHAPTER 12

NOT FINISHED YET—- "THE FUTURE LOOKS BRIGHT."

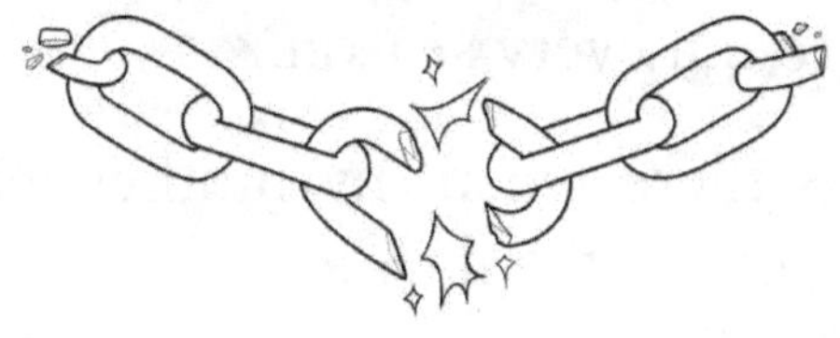

"He who began a good work in you will carry it on to completion..." Philippians 1:6 NIV

If there is one thing my life has taught me, it is this: God is not afraid of broken beginnings.

He is not intimidated by dysfunction, by generational pain, by the mistakes we make when we are searching for love in all the wrong places. He is not surprised by our failures, nor does He walk away when we fall short. Instead, He steps in—quietly, patiently, faithfully—working in ways we often cannot see until much later.

When I look back over my life, I no longer see a collection of disconnected events. I see a thread. A steady, unbroken thread of grace woven through every season.

He was there when my mother was a little girl crying out in the dark.

He was there in the chaos of my childhood.

He was there in every relationship that broke me and every door that closed.

He was there the night I cried out, "God, I need You," not knowing that He had been waiting for that moment all along.

And He is still here.

Still writing.

Still restoring.

Still redeeming.

I used to think my story was defined by what I went through—by the pain, the rejection, the mistakes, the things I wish I could undo. But now I understand that my story is not defined by what broke me…

It is defined by Who rebuilt me.

Because of Him, I am no longer the little girl searching for safety.

I am no longer the young woman looking for love in places that could never hold me.

I am no longer the version of myself that lived in fear, confusion, or shame.

I am becoming who He always intended me to be.

And that process is still unfolding.

There are still areas of my life He is shaping. Still places He is healing. Still lessons He is teaching me about love, humility, obedience, and faith.

Because redemption is not a moment—it is a journey.

A daily surrender.

A continual transformation.

A lifelong relationship with a God who refuses to leave His work unfinished.

And that is where my hope rests.

Not in perfection.

Not in having everything figured out.

But in knowing that the same God who carried me through every broken place in my life…

Is still carrying me forward.

So this is not the end of my story.

It is simply a place to pause.

To reflect.

To give thanks.

And to trust that what God has started in me, He will continue to complete.

Because I am living proof of this truth:

Even the most broken stories can be redeemed.

Even the deepest wounds can be healed.

Even the longest journeys can lead you home.

And by His grace—

I am not finished yet…

* * *

www.ingramcontent.com/pod-product-compliance
Lightning Source LLC
LaVergne TN
LVHW020650100826
845148LV00012B/2417

* 9 7 8 1 7 3 4 8 9 3 6 2 5 *